Which Instrument Will She Play?

by Laura T. Johnson

HOUGHTON MIFFLIN HARCOURT

PHOTOGRAPHY CREDITS: COVER ©Jose Luis Pelaez Inc/Blend Images/Getty Images; ©HMH; 3 (bl) ©Jose Luis Pelaez Inc/Blend Images/Getty Images; 3 (cl) ©Creatas/Getty Images; 3 (cr) ©HMH; 3 (c) ©Eyewire/Getty Images; 4 (b) ©Kumar Sriskandan/Alamy Images; 5 (r) ©Artville/Getty Images; 7 (t) ©Getty Images; 7 (cr) ©Tetra Images/Tetra Images/Corbis; 8 (tr) ©Brand X Pictures/Getty Images; 9 (bc) ©Houghton Mifflin Harcourt; 9 (b) Photodisc/Getty Images; 10 (t) ©Monkey Business images/Getty Images; 11 (b) ©Chris Harris/Alamy Images; 12 (t) ©Mode Images/Alamy Images; 14 (b) ©Andriano/Shutterstock

Printed in Mexico

ISBN: 978-0-544-07293-0

9 10 0908 21 20 19 18 17

4500669238   A B C D E F G

Contents

Vocabulary

energy   vibrate

sound   pitch

Stretch Vocabulary

compression   volume

sound wave   percussion

Introduction

Olivia was finally in third grade—the grade in which students in her school could choose an instrument to learn. Olivia's brother, Matt, had learned to play the trumpet. Her sister, Nadia, had learned to play the flute. Now it was Olivia's turn.

When Olivia's dad asked Olivia what instrument she was going to choose, she first said, "The violin!" Then she said, "No, the drums." And shortly after that she said, "The accordion would be fun. I'll think I'll choose that."

Dad said, "We need to make a trip to the music store to learn more about instruments!"

How will Olivia choose an instrument?

Instruments and Energy

On the way to the store, Olivia's dad explained how instruments create sound. "Energy is the ability to make something move or change. Sound is a kind of energy that travels in waves you can hear. Sound waves are created when something vibrates, or moves back and forth quickly. This starts new vibrations in the surrounding air. That's why instruments are grouped by how they produce vibrations. So, let's explore instruments that way."

Her dad's suggestion didn't surprise Olivia. He loved to connect science to everyday life.

Musical instruments have different ways of making the vibrations that create sound.

Five Groups of Instruments

Olivia's dad said, "Some instruments create sound when their strings vibrate. Some instruments make sounds when the air inside them vibrates. Still others vibrate and produce sound when they are hit or tapped."

Olivia interrupted him and asked, "But how do they make different notes?"

"You'll see," answered her dad. "Let's begin with brass instruments. Matt plays the trumpet. That's one kind of brass instrument."

"What part of a trumpet vibrates?" asked Olivia.

"No part," replied her dad. "You play the trumpet by vibrating your lips. That makes the air inside vibrate, too."

When you strike a drum, it vibrates and starts sound waves traveling through the air.

Brass Instruments

Olivia wasn't surprised that all the brass instruments were made of shiny metal. However, she was surprised by the variety of shapes and sizes.

Dad picked up a trombone. He explained, "Vibrations make sound in all instruments. To play a brass instrument, you blow into a mouthpiece. As you blow, your lips vibrate. This vibration creates sound waves."

"But how do you change notes?" Olivia asked again.

"It depends on the instrument," replied her dad.

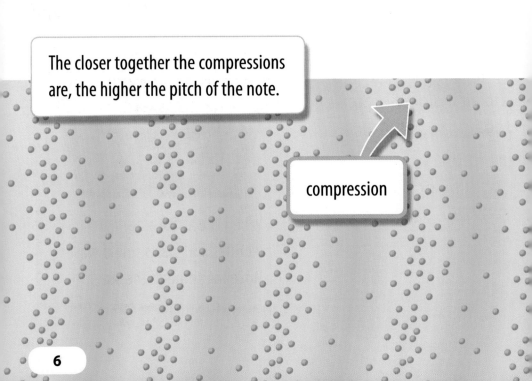

The closer together the compressions are, the higher the pitch of the note.

compression

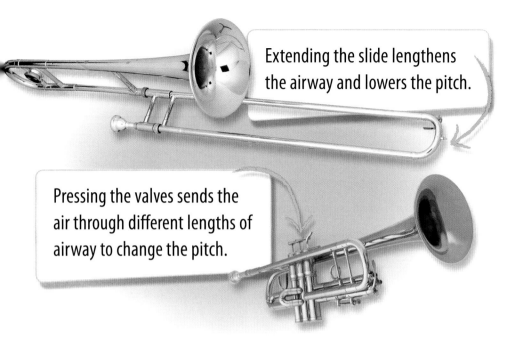

Extending the slide lengthens the airway and lowers the pitch.

Pressing the valves sends the air through different lengths of airway to change the pitch.

"Pitch describes how high or low a note is. When air vibrates more quickly, the compressions are closer together, and the note has a higher pitch. When air vibrates more slowly, the note has a lower pitch.

"The pitch of a brass or wind instrument depends on the length of the airway. The longer or shorter the airway, the lower or higher the pitch. A trombone player changes the length of the airway by moving a slide, a trumpet player by pressing one or more valves.

"Volume is how loud or soft a sound is. Changing how hard you blow into the instrument changes the volume."

Wind Instruments

Olivia's dad continued his explanation. "Wind instruments are played using your breath or 'wind.' Some wind instruments, like this clarinet, are called reed instruments. A reed is a very thin piece of wood. When a person blows into the mouthpiece, the reed vibrates and creates sound waves.

"To change notes, musicians press on keys to open or close holes in the instrument's tube. If all the holes are closed, the air vibrates through the whole length of the instrument. That produces low-pitched notes. Players open holes to make the airway shorter and raise the pitch."

"Isn't Nadia's flute a wind instrument?" asked Olivia. "It doesn't have a reed."

Look at the way the player is holding the keys. Is this for a low note or a high note?

"You're right!" said Olivia's dad. "Nadia blows air across the top of a hole in her flute. That makes the air inside the flute vibrate."

Then Olivia's dad picked up an instrument that looked like a small flute. "This is a piccolo. It's the same as a flute, but it's smaller. The notes have a much higher pitch. Can you tell me why?"

"Sure. It's smaller, so the air vibrates more quickly inside it. That makes a higher-pitched sound."

"Speaking of quick, you're a quick learner!" said her dad. "You're ready to move on to the strings."

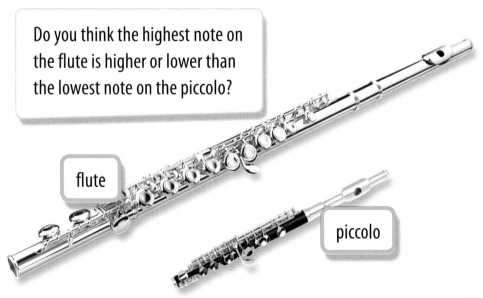

Do you think the highest note on the flute is higher or lower than the lowest note on the piccolo?

flute

piccolo

The bow of a stringed instrument is coated with a sticky material that makes the strings vibrate.

Stringed Instruments

"Like the others we've seen, stringed instruments use vibrations to make sound. You play these instruments by vibrating the strings." Olivia's dad moved from instrument to instrument, explaining how each one worked.

"Guitar players make the strings vibrate by plucking them with their fingers. Violin and cello players make the strings vibrate by moving a bow across them."

"How do stringed-instrument players change pitch?" asked Olivia.

Olivia's dad told Olivia to press a guitar string against the neck of the guitar. "Only the part of the string below your finger vibrates," he explained. "The shorter or tighter the vibrating section is, the faster it vibrates."

"And the faster it vibrates, the higher-pitched sound it makes," added Olivia.

"Right!" said her dad. "Now experiment with volume by strumming the strings harder and softer.

"We have two more instrument groups to explore. Let's go to the percussion section next."

Shortening the length of a vibrating string and tightening the string both raise the pitch. Why?

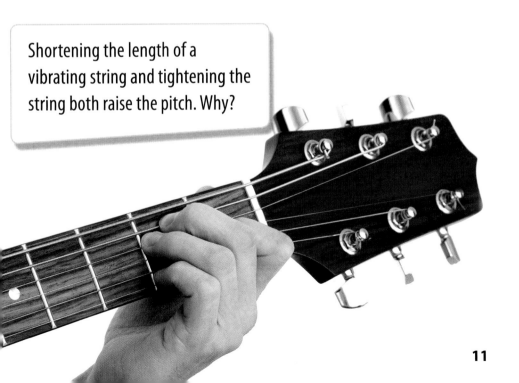

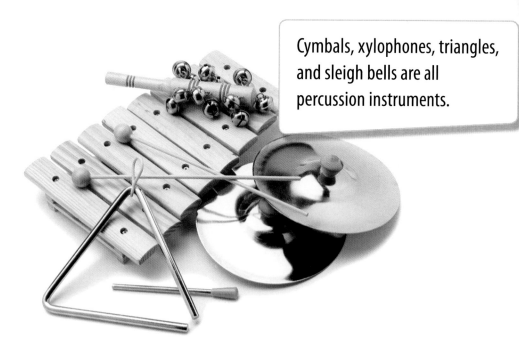

Cymbals, xylophones, triangles, and sleigh bells are all percussion instruments.

Percussion Instruments

"*Percussion* is a strange word. Why don't we just call this group 'drums?'" asked Olivia.

"*Percuss* means 'to strike or hit,'" her dad explained. "Percussion instruments vibrate when you hit or tap them. Drums are just one kind of percussion instrument.

"Many drums are made by stretching animal skins across the top of a cylinder. Drummers strike the skin with their hands or drumsticks to beat out rhythms and make notes."

"Drums make different notes?" asked Olivia in surprise.

"Yes, tightening and loosening the skin of the drum changes the drum's pitch. Tight skins vibrate more quickly and make a higher-pitched sound.

"Look around and you'll discover another reason why this section isn't called just 'the drums.' It also includes instruments like triangles, cymbals, and xylophones. They all make a sound when they're hit.

"Look the row of bars on this xylophone," said her dad. "Which one do you think makes the note with the highest-pitch?"

"The shortest one. It vibrates the fastest."

"Very good! We have one last group to explore."

What in this photograph tells you that the xylophone is a percussion instrument?

Pianos and Keyboards

"When you press a piano key, a hammer inside the piano strikes a string. This causes the string to vibrate," said Olivia's Dad.

"I know," said Olivia. "The shorter strings vibrate more quickly and make higher-pitched notes. The longer strings vibrate more slowly and make lower-pitched notes. Do electric keyboards make sound the same way?" asked Olivia.

"No. Let's save electronic instruments for another day! So, which kind of instrument do you want to learn?"

"A brass instrument! No. A wind instrument! Or maybe the drums?"

Is a piano a percussion instrument or a stringed instrument?

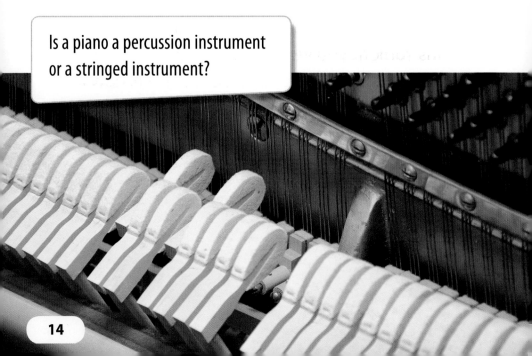

Experiment with Pitch

Make a drum to show how pitch changes. Place a sheet of plastic wrap over a bowl. Stretch a rubber band over the bowl to hold the plastic wrap in place. Gently stretch the wrap so it is tight and smooth. Strike it with a pen. Then loosen the plastic wrap so it is not stretched as tightly across the bowl. Tap it again. Describe how the pitch of the sound changed. Explain why it changed.

Describe an Invention

Write a paragraph describing a new musical instrument you would like to invent. Be sure to explain what the instrument looks like, how it produces vibrations, how the player changes the pitch, and what family of musical instruments your invention belongs to.

Glossary

compression [kuhm•PREH•shuhn] The part of a sound wave where the medium is compressed, or pushed.

energy [EN•er•jee] The ability to make something move or change.

percussion [per•KUH•shuhn] A kind of musical instrument that produces a sound when you hit or tap it.

pitch [PICH] How high or low a note or sound is.

sound [SOWND] Energy that travels in waves you can hear.

sound wave [SOWND WAYV] A flow of sound energy outward from its source.

vibrate [VY•brayt] To move quickly back and forth.

volume [VAHL•yoom] How loud or soft a sound is.